THE TIME MACHINE

Promit Hazra

pencil

ISBN 978-93-5458-713-9

Published in India 2021 by Pencil

A brand of
One Point Six Technologies Pvt. Ltd.
123, Building J2, Shram Seva Premises,
Wadala Truck Terminal, Wadala (E)
Mumbai 400037, Maharashtra, INDIA
E connect@thepencilapp.com
W www.thepencilapp.com

Author biography

This book is written By Promit Hazra,a writer from the city of joy,Kolkata,India. He is famous for some brilliant books : "The Virtual Death","Bastob O Rohosso (Bengali)" and many others. This book is based on the ancient age of India.

Promit Hazra born on 6th of June,2000 in the City, Howrah, located in West Bengal. He completed his secondary and Higher Secondary study from Santragachi Kadarnath Institution.

CONTENTS

Introduction

"Time Machine"-this is a mysterious thing. We all know that this machine is used for time travel. With this book we will travel through Indian History. In this 1st edition we will travel the ancient age of Indian History (From the Harappan Civilization to Rise of Magadha).

HISTORY OF HARAPPAN

Indus Valley civilization, also called Harappan civilization, the earliest known urban culture of the Indian subcontinent. The nuclear dates of the civilization appear to be about 2500–1700 BCE.

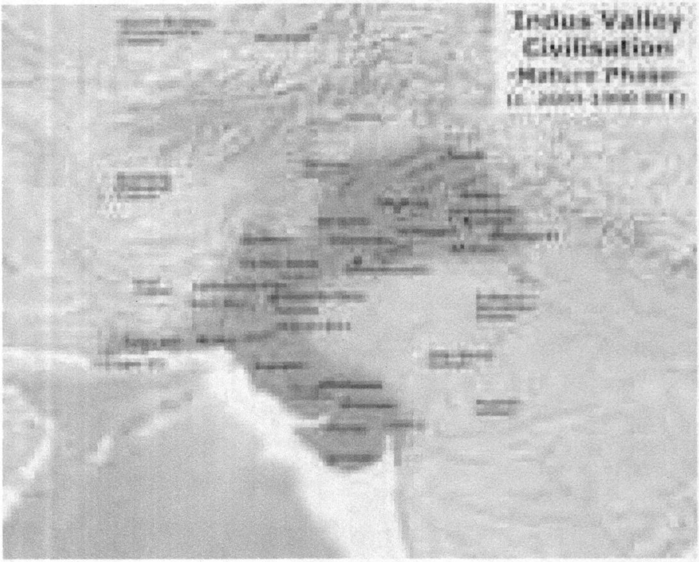

• **Origin and evolution :**The Harappan civilisation is dated between 2500 and 1700 BC. There were earlier and later cultures, known as Early Harappan and Later Harappan. The Harappan period characterised by seals, beads, weights, stone blades and baked bricks is called as the Mature Harappan culture.

- **Geography**: The Harappan civilisation was spread over Afghanistan, Sind, Beluchisthan, Jammu, Punjab, northern Rajasthan, Kathiawar and Gujarat. The Kalibangan-Mohenjo-Daro represent the centre of the Harappan civilisation. Most of the Harappan settlements were located in this region.The most remarkable feature of Harappan civilisation was its urbanisation. The Harappan places which were small towns, show an advanced sense of town planning. The major centres are Harappa, Mohenjo-Daro, Kalibangan, Lothal, Sutkagen-Dor, Dholavira, etc.Usually towns were laid out in a parallelogrammic form. Each towns was divided into a higher residential area where the essential institutions of civil and religious life were located and lower residential area where the urban population lived.System town planning, drainage system, granary, dockyard, public bathing place, use of bricks, buildings, etc. are some of the most impressive achievements of the Harappan civilisation.

- **Agriculture andCrafts**: The Harappan cultivated wheat and barley, peas and dates, sesame and mustard. In Lothal cultivated rice as early as 1800 BC. The evidence of a furrowed field in Kalibangan indicates that the Harappans used some sort of wooden plough. The irrigation depended on the irregular flooding of the rivers of Punjab and Sind.Various sculptures, seals, pottery, gold jewelry and figurines in terracotta, bronze and steatite, etc, have been excavated from the sites of the Harappan civilisation. Other crafts that have been unearthed include shell works, ceramics, agate, glazed steatite bead making, special kind of combs, etc. The dancing girl and the bearded head from Mohenjo-Daro are the two well known pieces of art.

- **Science**:The Harappans knew metal working and mining and constructing well planned multi storey buildings. They also knew to make long lasting paints and dyes.

- **Administration**: It is not clear as to what sort of political administration the Harappans had. However the sheer range and volume of products utilised by the residents of the larger towns indicate a centralised authority, possibly which could be a class of merchants.

- **Religion**:The various clay figures indicated that the Harappans worshipped the mother Goddess as the symbol of fertility. Certain trees seem to have been considered as sacred. Some people buried their dead in graves. The Harappans probably believed life after death, as their graves often contained household pottery, ornaments and mirrors belonging to the dead persons

THE VEDIC PERIOD

The Vedic Age is the "heroic age" of ancient Indian civilization. It is also the formative period when the basic foundations of Indian civilization were laid down. These include the emergence of early Hinduism as the foundational religion of India, and the social/religious phenomenon known as caste.This period of India's history lasted from around 1500 BCE through to 500 BCE; that is, from the early days of the Aryan migration into north-west India through to the age of the Buddha.

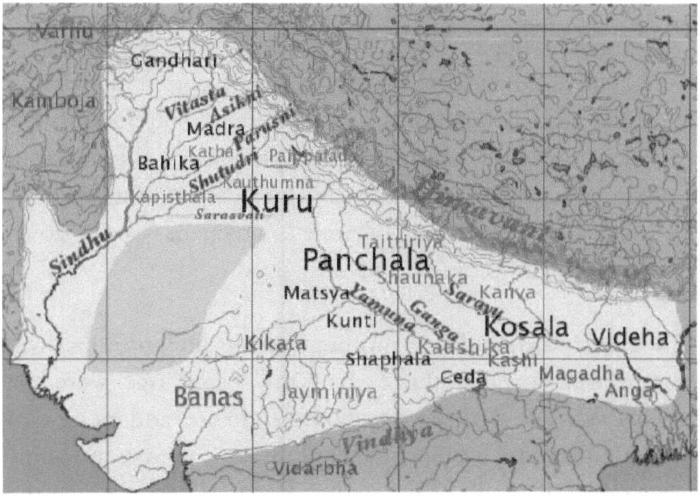

• **The Vedas :** The Aryans were a people from central Asia who spoke an Indo-European language. They brought with them into India a religion based on the worship of many gods and goddesses. This ancient religion is depicted in collections of oral poetry and prose – hymns, prayers, chants, spells and commentaries – known as the "Vedas".The Aryan belief-system that the Vedas reflect was distantly-related to those held by other Indo-European peoples of the ancient world, such as the Greeks and the Germans. However, some time in the centuries before they had entered India, the practice of fire ceremonies of the god Agni had become a focal part of their worship, a trait which they shared with their near-relatives, the Iranians (the word "Iranian" comes from the same root as the word "Aryan"). Another leading god was Indra, the High God. Also, the concept of the "Cycle of Life" – reincarnation of the soul from one earthly life to another – also arose in this period.The Aryans came into north-west India as pastoral, semi-nomadic tribes led by warrior chieftains. Once in India, they settled down as rulers over the native Dravidian populations they found there, and formed tribal kingdoms.The different kingdoms were often at war with one another, and echoes of these violent times can still be heard in one of the greatest epics of ancient India, the "Mahabharata", which has come down to us from this period of history

.• **TheUpanishads**: Another body of literature that was composed towards the end of the Vedic Age were the "Upanishads". The 200 sections of prose and poetry of which they are composed explore concepts only dimly perceived, if at all, in the earlier Vedas. These include the idea that the material world is unreal – indeed, it is an illusion. So too are Earthly emotions such as desire and suffering.To break the weary cycle of reincarnation which all souls have to go through, therefore, involves renouncing desire and other human feelings which bind the soul to the material world. This will allow the soul to be united with the "Brahma", and so achieve peace.These ideas helped to give the religious thought of ancient India a very distinctive flavour. They have influenced Indian civilization throughout its long history, right up to the present day.

• **Born of Hindu Religion and Caste System :** The Vedas, the Mahabharata and the Upanishads formed the foundational writings of the Hindu religion, which was gradually taking shape in the Vedic Age. They show that the ancient Vedic religion was evolving into something different. This was probably to a large extent the result of influences from the older Dravidian populations over whom the Aryans ruled. During the course of centuries the Aryan nature deities lost much of their importance, and three new gods took their place: Vishnu, the preserver; Shiva, the destroyer; and Brahma, the creator.The ideas associated with the Upanishads became important, and these had a profound effect on social life. The notion that every element of creation – humans, animals, plants, rocks and so on – had a portion of the World Soul dwelling in them ("Atman") gained acceptance within ancient Indian society. With it came a respect for all living things.It was during this period of history that ancient India developed its distinctive caste system.The tendencies towards social division had been present ever since the coming of Aryans into India. As happened at many different times and places in world history, the conquerors set themselves up as a ruling class. However, unlike in other parts of the world, where the differences between the conquerors and the conquered gradually disappeared over time, in India they solidified in the form of divisions between the castes, between whom intermarriage was forbidden.The priestly caste – the Brahmins – were at the top of the social ladder, as being closest to Brahma. Below them came the warrior caste, the Kshatryas. Then came the Vaishyas, the ordinary Aryan tribesmen, farmers, craftsmen and traders. Finally came the Shudras, menial workers, the laborers, servants and those performing services which are ritually unclean. There were also many people outside the caste system altogether, excluded from Aryan-dominated society. These were called the "Untouchables". They were not really regarded as human beings, and performed the most degrading tasks of all, such as dealing with human waste.

• **The rebirth of urban civilization :** As the Vedic Age drew to a close, the tribal society of the early Aryans gave way to a more complex social organization. The use of iron spread from the Middle East from around 800 BCE. This made agriculture more productive, and populations grew. Trade expanded, both within India and with the lands to the west. From the Middle East came the use of writing, and the great oral traditions of Aryan society began to be written down. Organized kingdoms with centralised authority emanating out from the royal palaces arose in place of the looser, clan-based tribal states. Not just kingdoms, either; in some places, particularly in the mountain areas and on the fringes of the Aryan world (essentially present-day modern Pakistan and northern and north-central India), confederations of clan-chiefs arose which later generations have labelled "republics". This makes ancient India the only place (as far as we know) in which the republican form of government flourished in the ancient world apart from in the Classical world of the ancient Mediterranean.

BUDDHISM

Buddhism is a faith that was founded by Siddhartha Gautama ("the Buddha") more than 2,500 years ago in India. With about 470 million followers, scholars consider Buddhism one of the major world religions.

A gold Buddha figure at the Longhua Temple in the south of Shanghai, first built in 242 AD.

- **History :** Siddhartha Gautama, the founder of Buddhism who later became known as "the Buddha," lived during the 5th century B.C. Gautama was born into a wealthy family as a prince in present-day Nepal. Although he had an easy life, Gautama was moved by suffering in the world. He decided to give up his lavish lifestyle and endure poverty. When this didn't fulfill him, he promoted the idea of the "Middle Way," which means existing between two extremes. Thus, he sought a life without social indulgences but also without deprivation.After six years of searching, Buddhists believe Gautama found enlightenment while meditating under a Bodhi tree. He spent the rest of his life teaching others about how to achieve this spiritual state.When Gautama passed away around 483 B.C., his followers began to organize a religious movement. Buddha's teachings became the foundation for what would develop into Buddhism.In the 3rd century B.C., Ashoka the Great, the Mauryan Indian emperor, made Buddhism the state religion of India. Buddhist monasteries were built, and missionary work was encouraged.Over the next few centuries, Buddhism began to spread beyond India. The thoughts and philosophies of Buddhists became diverse, with some followers interpreting ideas differently than others.In the sixth century, the Huns invaded India and destroyed hundreds of Buddhist monasteries, but the intruders were eventually driven out of the country.Islam began to spread quickly in the region during the Middle Ages, forcing Buddhism into the background.

- **Types of Buddhism :**Theravada Buddhism: Prevalent in Thailand, Sri Lanka, Cambodia, Laos and BurmaMahayana Buddhism: Prevalent in China, Japan, Taiwan, Korea, Singapore and VietnamTibetan Buddhism: Prevalent in Tibet, Nepal, Mongolia, Bhutan, and parts of Russia and northern IndiaEach of these types reveres certain texts and has slightly different interpretations of Buddha's teachings. There are also several subsects of

Buddhism, including Zen Buddhism and Nirvana Buddhism.Some forms of Buddhism incorporate ideas of other religions and philosophies, such as Taoism and Bon.

• **Dharma :** Buddha's teachings are known as "dharma." He taught that wisdom, kindness, patience, generosity and compassion were important virtues.Specifically, all Buddhists live by five moral precepts, which prohibit:*Killing living thingsTaking what is not givenSexual misconductLyingUsing drugs or alcohol*

• **Four Noble Truths :** The Four Noble Truths, which Buddha taught, are:

◆ The truth of suffering (dukkha)

◆ The truth of the cause of suffering (samudaya)

◆ The truth of the end of suffering (nirhodha)

◆ The truth of the path that frees us from suffering (magga)Collectively, these principles explain why humans hurt and how to overcome suffering.

• **Eightfold Path :** The Buddha taught his followers that the end of suffering, as described in the fourth Noble Truths, could be achieved by following an Eightfold Path. In no particular order, the Eightfold Path of Buddhism teaches the following ideals for ethical conduct, mental disciple and achieving wisdom:

◆ Right understanding (Samma ditthi)

◆ Right thought (Samma sankappa)

◆ Right speech (Samma vaca)

◆ Right action (Samma kammanta)

◆ Right livelihood (Samma ajiva)

◆ Right effort (Samma vayama)

◆ Right mindfulness (Samma sati)

◆ Right concentration (Samma samadhi)

• **Buddhism Beliefs :**Some key Buddhism beliefs include:

◆ Followers of Buddhism don't acknowledge a supreme god or deity. They instead focus on achieving enlightenment—a state of inner peace and wisdom. When followers reach this spiritual echelon, they're said to have experienced nirvana.

◆ The religion's founder, Buddha, is considered an extraordinary man, but not a god. The word Buddha means "enlightened."

◆ The path to enlightenment is attained by utilizing morality, meditation and wisdom. Buddhists often meditate because they believe it helps awaken truth.

◆ There are many philosophies and interpretations within

Buddhism, making it a tolerant and evolving religion.Some scholars don't recognize Buddhism as an organized religion, but rather, a "way of life" or a "spiritual tradition."

◆ Buddhism encourages its people to avoid self-indulgence but also self-denial.Buddha's most important teachings, known as The Four Noble Truths, are essential to understanding the religion.Buddhists embrace the concepts of karma (the law of cause and effect) and reincarnation (the continuous cycle of rebirth).

◆ Followers of Buddhism can worship in temples or in their own homes.Buddhist monks, or bhikkhus, follow a strict code of conduct, which includes celibacy.

◆ There is no single Buddhist symbol, but a number of images have evolved that represent Buddhist beliefs, including the lotus flower, the eight-spoked dharma wheel, the Bodhi tree and the swastika (an ancient symbol whose name means "well-being" or "good fortune" in Sanskrit).

• Buddhist Holy Book : Buddhists revere many sacred texts and scriptures. Some of the most important are:

◆ Tipitaka: These texts, known as the "three baskets," are thought to be the earliest collection of Buddhist writings.

◆ Sutras: There are more than 2,000 sutras, which are sacred teachings embraced mainly by Mahayana Buddhists.

◆ The Book of the Dead: This Tibetan text describes the stages of death in detail.

JAINISM

Jainism is an ancient religion that is rooted in the philosophy that teaches the way to liberation and a path to spiritual purity and enlightenment through disciplined nonviolence to all living creatures.

23rd Tirthankara Parsvanatha, Madhya Pradesh, Central India, 7th century. Sandstone sculpture. Museum no. IS.18-1956

- **About Jainism :**

Jainism, one of the three major religions of early India, has been continuously practised since around the middle of the first millennium BC. Its name derives from the word Jina, meaning 'liberator' or 'victor', referring to spiritual rather than material conquest. Jains believe (as do Buddhists and Hindus) in a cycle of birth and rebirth, influenced by the effects of the individual's actions and attitudes (a concept known as 'karma'). The ultimate goal of the believer is to break the cycle and achieve liberation. To help them achieve this goal, Jains revere a group of 24 liberated souls called Jinas or Tirthankaras ('those who ford the river' between the material and spiritual worlds), who act as teachers and role models to the faithful.

The Jain system also includes various gods, goddesses and protective deities who serve the Jinas and are often the focus of independent cults. Unlike the Jinas, these secondary deities are capable of divine intervention, granting boons for the devotee.

There are currently some six million followers worldwide. Jainism has long been respected as the world's most peace-loving religion because of its strict doctrine of non-violence (ahimsa). Mahatma Gandhi, born a Hindu, was an admirer of Jainism's teachings and adopted the doctrine of non-violence in his movement for Indian independence.

The Jains' commitment to non-violence and non-possession limits the types of lay occupations they can pursue. They have traditionally been traders and merchants in textile, jewellery and financial businesses, and today are also prominent in medicine and technical industries. The Jain community's prosperity has long enabled them to be generous patrons. In India today we can see the monuments, stone sculptures, images in bronze and wood and the temple libraries which house the sacred literature. They all bear witness to the fruitful tradition of Jain patronage and artistic achievement.

- **The Peaceful Liberators :**

The Jains employ numerous symbolic and ritual objects to give expression to important aspects of their religion. The earliest surviving Jain ritual objects are carved stone tablets, which were decorated with auspicious symbols (ayagapata). Later, Jain objects began to incorporate more philosophical themes. The 'bodiless' silhouette images, for example, symbolised liberated beings beyond corporeal form.

The Jains observe two principal festivals in their religious calendar. The first is Diwali, the festival of lights, which marks the release (moksha) from the cycle of rebirth of Mahavira, the most recent Jina. The lighting of candles is intended to dispel the darkness created by his departure. The second is Paryushan, traditionally held at the beginning of India's rainy season in September, a time when the monsoons restrict travel and activity. It is the festival of forgiveness, when Jains retire to repent, fast and meditate.

Western commentators have not always understood the distinctive identity of Jainism or, indeed, acknowledged its role in the building of India's artistic heritage. Jainism is often defined in terms of comparisons with Buddhism and Hinduism. While these religions share a common heritage, and in some cases share deities and even iconography, Jain teachings represent a different and separate religious tradition. Jain objects and paintings are often adorned with pictographic emblems of the fourteen auspicious dreams of Mahavira's mother, foretelling the spiritual superiority of Mahavira.

Other emblems include the eight auspicious signs, symbolic of various Jain concepts. Representations of the celestial assembly of the Jinas also feature, as do images of the mythical continents which they inhabit.

- **The emergence of Jainism :**

In the first half of the first millennium BC, the dominant religious system in northern India was based on the Vedic scriptures. The concept of sacrificial ritual, presided over by brahmin priests, specialist intermediaries between men and gods, was at its centre. Through the officiating priests and complex rites, people used animal sacrifice to win benefits from the gods. In about the sixth century BC, towns began to appear, along with the economic and social changes that accompanied this urbanisation.

Very broadly around the same time, new forms of religious thought and practice were emerging, both within and outside the Vedic system. A new emphasis developed on escaping the cycle of rebirth. Jainism, along with Buddhism, emerged in a milieu in which religious seekers renounced the life of the householder to become wandering mendicants. Both Mahavira and the Buddha belonged to this tradition. They were born into the warrior caste (ksatriya), and lived in eastern India, in an area of the Ganges valley including the modern state of Bihar. The new thinkers questioned the dominant Vedic Brahmanical orthodoxy (in which an entity called brahman was considered supreme) and its stratified caste system with brahmins (priests) at the top. They rejected animal sacrifice. For Jains in particular, a central tenet of their faith was a renunciation of violence in all its forms and a concern for all forms of life.

- **Beliefs and philosophy**:

The hand symbolizes Ahiṃsā, the wheel dharmachakra, the resolve to halt saṃsāra (transmigration).

Jainism is transtheistic and forecasts that the universe evolves without violating the law of substance dualism,auto executed through the middle ground between the principles of parallelism and interactionism.

◆ **Dravya (Substance) :**

Dravya means substances or entity in Sanskrit. According to Jain philosophy, the universe is made up of six eternal substances: sentient beings or souls (jīva), non-sentient substance or matter (pudgala), principle of motion (dharma), the principle of rest (adharma), space (ākāśa) and time (kāla). The latter five are united as the ajiva (the non-living). Jain philosophers distinguish a substance from a body, or thing, by declaring the former a simple indestructible element, while the latter is a compound, made of one or more substances, which can be destroyed.

◆ **Tattva (Reality) :**

Tattva connotes reality or truth in Jain philosophy, and is the framework for salvation. According to Digambara Jains, there are seven tattvas: the sentient (jiva)living; the insentient (ajiva)non-living; the karmic influx to the soul (Āsrava)Mix of Living and non living; bondage of karmic particles to the soul (Bandha);stoppage of karmic particles (Saṃvara); wiping away of past karmic particles (Nirjarā); and liberation (Moksha). Śvētāmbaras add two further tattvas, namely good karma (Punya) and bad karma (Paap).

The true insight in Jain philosophy is considered as "faith in the tattvas". The spiritual goal in Jainism is to reach moksha for ascetics, but for most Jain laypersons it is to accumulate good karma that leads to better rebirth and a step closer to liberation.

◆ Soul and karma :

According to Jainism, the existence of "a bound and ever changing soul" is a self-evident truth, an axiom which does not need to be proven. It maintains that there are numerous souls, but every one of them has three qualities (Guṇa): consciousness (caitanya, the most important), bliss (sukha) and vibrational energy (virya). It further claims that the vibration draws karmic particles to the soul and creates bondages, but is also what adds merit or demerit to the soul. Jain texts state that souls exist as "clothed with material bodies", where it entirely fills up the body.Karma, as in other Indian religions, connotes in Jainism the universal cause and effect law. However, it is envisioned as a material substance (subtle matter) that can bind to the soul, travel with the soul in bound form between rebirths, and affect the suffering and happiness experienced by the jiva in the lokas. Karma is believed to obscure and obstruct the innate nature and striving of the soul, as well as its spiritual potential in the next rebirth.

◆ Saṃsāra :

The conceptual framework of the Saṃsāra doctrine differs between Jainism and other Indian religions. Soul (jiva) is accepted as a truth, as in Hinduism but not Buddhism. The cycle of rebirths has a definite beginning and end in Jainism. Jain theosophy asserts that each soul passes through 8,400,000 birth-situations as they circle through Saṃsāra,going through five types of bodies: earth bodies, water bodies, fire bodies, air bodies and vegetable lives, constantly changing with all human and non-human activities from rainfall to breathing.

◆ God :

Jainism is a transtheistic religion,holding that the universe was not created, and will exist forever. It is believed to be independent, having no creator, governor, judge, or destroyer. In this, it is unlike the Abrahamic religions, but similar to Buddhism. However, Jainism believes in the world of heavenly and hell beings who are born, die and reborn like earthly beings. Jain texts maintain that souls who live happily in the body of a god do so because of their positive karma. It is further stated that they possess a more transcendent knowledge about material things and can anticipate events in the human realms. However, once their past karmic merit is exhausted, it is explained that their souls are reborn again as humans, animals or other beings. In Jainism, perfect souls with a body are called arihant (victors) and perfect souls without a body are called Siddhas (liberated souls).

◆ Epistemology :

Jain philosophy accepts three reliable means of knowledge (pramana). It holds that correct knowledge is based on perception (pratyaksa), inference (anumana) and testimony (sabda or the word of scriptures). These ideas are elaborated in Jain texts such as Tattvarthasūtra, Parvacanasara, Nandi and Anuyogadvarini. Some Jain texts add analogy (upamana) as the fourth reliable means, in a manner similar to epistemological theories found in other Indian religions. In Jainism, jnāna (knowledge) is said to be of five kinds – Kevala Jnana (Omniscience), Śrutu Jñāna (Scriptural Knowledge), Mati Jñāna (Sensory Knowledge), Avadhi Jñāna (Clairvoyance), and Manah prayāya Jñāna (Telepathy). According to the Jain text Tattvartha sūtra, the first two are indirect knowledge and the remaining three are direct knowledge.

◆ Cosmology :

Jain texts propound that the universe consists of many eternal lokas (realms of existence). As in Buddhism and Hinduism, both time and the universe are eternal, but the universe is transient. The universe, body, matter and time are considered separate from the soul (jiva). Their interaction explains life, living, death and rebirth in Jain philosophy. The Jain cosmic universe has three parts, the upper, middle, and lower worlds (urdhva loka, madhya loka, and adho loka). Jainism states that Kāla (time) is without beginning and eternal; the cosmic wheel of time, kālachakra, rotates ceaselessly. In this part of the universe, it explains, there are six periods of time within two eons (ara), and in the first eon the universe generates, and in the next it degenerates. Thus, it divides the worldly cycle of time into two half-cycles, utsarpiṇī (ascending, progressive prosperity and happiness) and avasarpiṇī (descending, increasing sorrow and immorality). It states that the world is currently in the fifth ara of avasarpiṇī, full of sorrow and religious decline, where the height of living beings shrinks. According to Jainism, after the sixth era, the universe will be reawakened in a new cycle.

◆ **Salvation, liberation :**

According to Jainism, purification of soul and liberation can be achieved through the path of four jewels:

Samyak darśana (Correct View), meaning faith, acceptance of the truth of soul (jīva);

Samyak gyana (Correct Knowledge), meaning undoubting knowledge of the tattvas;

Samyak charitra (Correct Conduct), meaning behavior consistent with the Five vows. Jain texts often add samyak tap (Correct Asceticism) as a fourth jewel, emphasizing belief in ascetic practices as the means to liberation (moksha). The four jewels are called moksha marg (the path of liberation).

RISE OF SIXTEEN MAHAJANAPADAS

The Mahajanapadas were a set of sixteen kingdoms that existed in ancient India. It all began when the tribes (janas) of the late Vedic period decided to form their own territorial communities, which eventually gave rise to new and permanent areas of settlements called 'states' or 'janapadas.' In the sixth century BC, present-day Bihar and eastern Uttar Pradesh became centers of political activities as the region was not only fertile but also closer to the iron production centers. Iron production played a crucial role in expanding the territorial states of the region. These expansions helped some of these 'janapadas' turn into large states or 'mahajanapadas.' Most of these 'mahajanapadas' were monarchical in nature, while some of them were democratic states. Many prominent ancient Buddhist texts make frequent references to the '16 great kingdoms' (mahajanapadas) that flourished between the sixth and the fourth centuries BCE. These 16 kingdoms included kingdoms like Anga, Gandhara, Kuru, and Panchala, which are mentioned in the great Indian epic 'Mahabharata.'

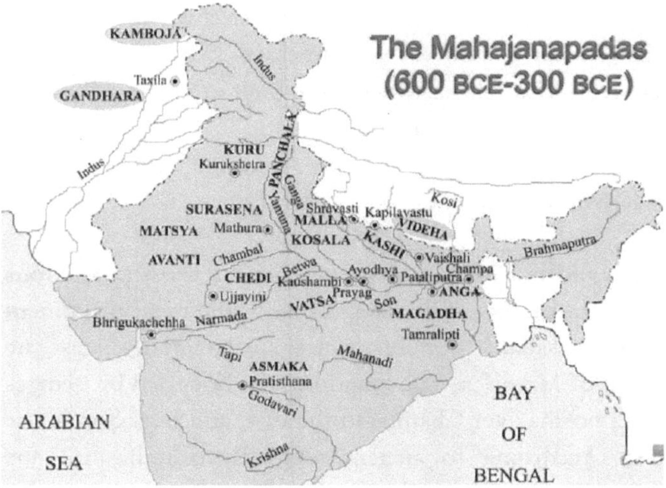

• **History of the Mahajanapadas :** In order to settle down permanently, simple land-grabbing process was started by the tribes, which eventually turned into well-planned communities. These communities gave rise to states or 'janapadas' and tribal identity became a major factor in defining the territory of a particular state. Gradually, some of these states began to expand and hence came to be known as the 'mahajanapadas.' Since expansion involved annexing of neighbouring states, certain 'mahajanapadas' started conquering other 'janapadas' in order to extend their kingdoms as per the kingdom's prosperity and wealth.Early stages of settlement of the tribes happened before the time of the Buddha. Hence, historical references of these 'mahajanapadas' can be found in ancient Buddhist texts. Many such texts talk about '16 great kingdoms' that flourished between the sixth and the fourth centuries BCE. The period between the sixth and fourth centuries BCE is considered extremely important in early Indian history as it witnessed the emergence of massive Indian cities, which were built after the fall of the Indus Valley Civilization.

- **16 Mahajanapadas**:

1. Magadha : Magadha was one of the most prosperous kingdoms of ancient India and one of the most prominent 'mahajanapadas.' For many years, Pataliputra was the capital of Magadha. The kingdom was bounded by Ganges in the north, river Champa in the east, and river Son in the west. According to ancient texts, Brihadratha was the earliest known ruler of Magadha. The kingdom was also ruled by King Bimbisara, under whom Magadha flourished. Great Indian empires including the famous Maurya Dynasty originated in Magadha. Gautama Buddha spent much of his life in Magadha, hence the region is believed to hold great significance to Buddhists.

2. Gandhara : According to Hecataeus of Miletus, Purushapura or present-day Peshawar served as a grand Gandharic city. Other references pertaining to Gandhara have been made in ancient texts like 'Rigveda,' 'Ramayana,' and 'Mahabharata.' This great kingdom was served graciously by river Indus and its capital Taksashila (Taxila) housed the renowned center of learning, the 'Taksashila University.' Scholars came to the university from all over the world in order to seek greater knowledge and wisdom. Though Gandhara was a huge kingdom on its own, it is often considered to be a part of an empire by modern-day scholars. Dr. T. L. Shah even argued that Gandhara and

Kamboja, which was one of the 16 'mahajanapadas,' were two provinces of a single empire.

3. Kamboja : The state of Kamboja is referred to as republican in several ancient scripts. These scripts also state that there were two Kamboja settlements, a theory which is backed by modern-day historians. It is said that ancient Kamboja was located on either sides of the Hindukush mountain range. But clans of Kamboja are believed to have crossed the mountain range to plant colonies in the southern side as well. These clans of people are associated with the Gandharas and Daradas and find mention in many Indian texts, including the edicts of Ashoka the Great.

4. Kuru : At the time of the Budhha, Kuru was ruled by Korayvya, a titular chieftain. Its capital was Indraprastha (present-day Delhi), which was known for people with sound health and deep wisdom. The Kurus were related to people of other communities like the 'Panchalas' and the 'Yadavas' as they had matrimonial relations with them. Though Kuru kingdom was a well-known monarchical state in the ancient world, the 6th and 5th centuries BCE saw the formation of republican form of government in the land of Kuru. Kautiliya's 'Arthashastra,' which was written in Sanskrit in the 4th century BCE, also states that the Kurus followed the king consul constitution.

5. Kosala : The kingdom of Kosala was located close to the kingdom of Magadha. With Ayodhya as its capital, Kosala was bound by river Ganges in the south, river Gandak in the east, and the Himalaya mountains in the north. According to Vedic texts, Kosala was the biggest and most powerful kingdom ever in history. At the time of the Buddha and Mahavira, Kosala kingdom was ruled by King Prasenajit. After a series of tactical moves for supremacy by Kosala and Magadha, the kingdom of Kosala was eventually merged with Magadha, when Kosala was being ruled by Vidudabha.

6. Malla : The Mallas of the Malla kingdom are often described as powerful people who dwelled in Northern South Asia. Many Buddhist texts refer to the kingdom as a republican dominion made up of nine territories. Like Kuru, Malla kingdom too had monarchical forms of government, but later moved towards the republican form of government. Ancient cities like Kusinara and Pava, which belonged to the Malla kingdom, are considered extremely important by Jains and Buddhists. While Lord Mahavira had his last meal at Kusinara, Gauthama Buddha had his last meal at Pava. Both Kusinara and Pava are believed to have hosted Buddha for a long period of time.

7. Panchala : The Panchala kingdom was located east of the Kuru kingdom, between river Ganges and the mountain ranges of the Himalayas. Panchala was divided into two parts, namely Dakshina-Panchala and Uttara-Panchala. While Adhichhatra (present-day Bareilly) served as the capital city of Uttara-Panchala, Kampilya (present-day Farrukhabad) was made the capital of Dakshina-Panchala. Originally a monarchical kingdom, Panchala is believed to have turned into a republican dominion during the 6th and 5th centuries BCE. Kautiliya's 'Arthashastra' also states that Panchala followed the king consul constitution. The kingdom was later annexed by Mauryan Empire and then by the Gupta Empire.

8. Matsya : Located south to the Kuru kingdom and west to river Yamuna, the Matsya kingdom was founded by an Indo-Aryan tribe of Vedic age. Apart from serving as the main water source, Yamuna also separated Matsya kingdom from the Panchalas. Viratanagara (present-day Bairat), which was named after the kingdom's founder Virata, was Matsya's capital. According to ancient texts, a king named Sujata ruled over Matsya as well as Chedi, which later became a separate kingdom. Though Matsya is mentioned as one of the 'mahajanapadas' in various Buddhist texts, its political power had greatly dwindled by the time of the Buddha.

9. Chedi : The kingdom of Chedi finds great prominence in the Hindu epic Mahabharata. According to the ancient text, Chedi was ruled by a king named Shishupala, who was an ally of the kings from Magadha and Kuru. A city named Suktimati has been described as the kingdom's capital. Though the exact location of modern-day Suktimati has not been figured out yet, prominent historians like F. E. Pargiter and Hem Chandra Raychaudhuri say that the ancient city might have been established near present-day Banda in Uttar Pradesh. An Indian archaeologist named Dilip Kumar Chakrabarti has claimed that the ruins of a historical city near the outskirts of Rewa in Madhya Pradesh may unlock further details pertaining to the kingdom and its capital city.

10. Anga : The earliest references to the people of Anga are made in the 'Atharva Veda,' which describes the Angas as despised people. The 'Jaina Prajnapana' claims that Angas were among the earliest groups of Aryan people. Over a period of time, the kingdom of Anga became a great center of trade, attracting merchants from the neighboring kingdoms. Anga and its rival Magadha were separated by river Champa, which served as the main water source for both the kingdoms. Anga was eventually annexed by Magadha in King Bimbisara's one and only conquest.

11. Avanti : Post Mahavira and Buddha, the kingdom of Avanti was considered as one of the four great monarchies along with Kosala, Magadha, and Vatsa. Apart from serving as the kingdom's principal source of water, river Narmada also separated Avanti into two parts – North Avanti and South Avanti. However, North and South Avanti were integrated at the time of Buddha and Mahavira, during which Ujjaini served as the common capital of the integrated kingdom. Avanti was a great center of Buddhism. When King Shishunaga defeated Nandivardhana, Avanti became a part of Magadha.

12. Vatsa : Vatsa or Vamsa, which was located near the present-day Allahabad in Uttar Pradesh, thrived under a monarchical form of government. King Udayana of the 7th century BCE ruled Vatsa with Kausambi as its capital. Though Udayana initially opposed the teachings of the Buddha, he became a follower of Buddha later in his life and even made Buddhism as the state religion of Kausambi. Vatsa's capital city attracted a number of wealthy merchants, who made Kausambi their home.

Kausambi was also a prominent entreport of passengers and goods, coming in from the south and north-west.

13. Assaka : The Kingdom of Assaka was located in southern India. Apart from serving as the kingdom's principal source of water, river Godavari separated Assaka from Mulaka, which was also known as Alaka. It is said that Mulaka was once a part of Assaka. According to Buddhist texts, King Brahmadatta ruled over Assaka with its capital at Potali (present-day Maharashtra). Assaka is described as one of the 16 'mahajanapadas' in an ancient Buddhist text known as 'Anguttara Nikaya.'

14. Surasena : The kingdom of Surasena was located to the west of river Yamuna and to the east of Matsya kingdom. Surasena played an important role in propagating Buddhism as the king of Surasena, Avantiputra, was among the earliest known chief disciples of Buddha. During the time of Megasthenes, Mathura, the capital of Surasena, was known as a city where worshipping Krishna was considered prominent. The kingdom of Surasena, which once flourished, was later annexed by the Magadhan Empire.

15. Vajji : Vajji was one of the most prominent 'mahajanapadas' of ancient India. Vajji finds mention in the Jaina text 'Bhagavati Sutra' and in Buddhist texts like 'Anguttara Nikaya.' Vajji was located towards the north of the river Ganges and was bound by river Gandaki in the west. Apart from serving as Vajji's chief source of water, river Gandaki is believed to have played a key role in separating Vajji from Malla and Kosala as well. Apart from

Vaishali, which was its capital city, Vajji also housed popular ancient cities like Hatthigama, Bhoganagara, and Kundapura.

16. Kashi : Ancient Kashi was bound by river Varuna in the north and river Assi in the south. The Kingdom of Kashi, which had its capital at Varanasi, was the most powerful among 'mahajanapadas' before the time of the Buddha. Several ancient texts speak highly of Kashi, which was one of the most prosperous kingdoms during its heyday. Hence, Kashi was in constant conflict with kingdoms of Kosala, Magadha, and Anga, which were trying to annex Kashi. Though Kosala was once defeated by Kashi, it was later annexed by Kosala under the rule of King Kansa, who ruled at the time of Buddha.

RISE OF MAGADHA

Magadha had to contend for political pre-eminence with the monarchical states of Kashi, Kosala and Vatsa. Besides, the republican confederacy of the Vrijis was also a strong contender. The struggle between them continued for about a century and. Ultimately, Magadha emerged victorious and established itself as the supreme power.

- **The Causes of the Rise of Magadha :**

◆ The kingdom of Magadha started its rise to pre-eminence during the period of Bimbisara and finally became the first great empire in India by the time of the Nandas. Various ambitious and powerful rulers of different successive dynasties contributed to its rise. But certain other geographical, economic and cultural factors also contributed to its rise. There were certain permanent factors which enabled it to rise to zenith of political greatness more than once. It remained the seat of power for many successive empires in India.

◆ Magadha occupied a strategic position of geographical importance. The river Ganges and its tributaries Son, Gandak and Gagra served as admirable means for defence, communication and trade. The older capital Rajagriha was protected by seven hills and the later one; Pataliputara being at the junction of the Ganges and the Son had natural means of defence.

◆ The natural facilities of communication and trade both with North India and the sea helped it in its economic prosperity. The land of Magadha was also fertile which yielded rich harvests. Therefore, land taxes could be kept high which proved to be regular and substantial sources of income to the state without which the maintenance of a big army could not be possible and the empire could neither be built up nor consolidated.

◆ The taxes Bali and Bhag had now become compulsory and the peasants had no choice but to pay them. The state imposed further taxes on labour and peasants and collected good money by trade-tax as well.

◆ Because of increased financial resources, Magadh was the first state in north India to keep a standing army and Bimbisara the first such ruler. Besides, while neighbouring forests provided timber for building and elephants for the army, its own iron-ore deposits made profitable the manufacture of better implements and weapons and a profitable trade in iron.

◆ Magadh was again the first state in India which manufactured better arms and equipment of war made of iron. All this helped in making Magadha an economically prosperous and militarily strong state which helped in its rise.

◆ Culturally, Magadha, being in the East, was a place where a balanced synthesis between the Aryan and the non-Aryan cultures took place. The Brahamanic culture could not claim dominance in Magadha because by the time it reached there it had lost much of its strength and therefore, liberal traditions in religion and society could be maintained in Magadha.

◆ Prof H.C. Ravchaudhari writes "In their realm Brahmanas could fraternize with Vratyas, Kshatriyas could admit plebian (Sudra) girls to their harem, blue-blooded aristocrats could be done to death or otherwise deprived of the throne to make room for the child of a 'Nagar-Sobhini' and a barber could aspire to imperial dignity."

◆ Jainism and Buddhism both of which took their birth within the territories of Magadha were, probably, the results of these liberal traditions and they participated in further enhancing these traditions "It (Magadha)," writes Prof H.C. Ravchaudhari, "played a part in the evolution of universal religion as it did in the foundation of a pan-Indian empire. " Liberal traditions, particularly a sense of social equality and catholicity of religious ideas, further strengthened by Jainism and Buddhism, also contributed to the building of a strong empire in Magadha.

◆ Dr Radha Kumud Mookerji writes, "The laxity of social restrictions imposed by the orthodox Brahmanical culture and universal aspect of Buddhism and Jainism which found a congenial home in the Magadha must have considerably widened the political outlook of this region and contributed to make it the nucleus of a mighty empire."

◆ The administrative system of Magadha, wherein the state was ruled by a hereditary monarch who had the opportunity to enhance his financial and military resources, was also one of the causes of its rise. The powers of the king had increased under monarchical-state. In the previous tribal-system, the king got only a part of the booty of the war. In the new system, he could keep it all for himself.

◆ The kings now, besides Bali, started collecting other taxes as well like Bhaga and Kara. They extorted money from their subjects by several illegal means also. All that made different states financially strong which enabled kings to maintain standing armies. Bimbisara of Magadha was the first king among monarchical states of that time who kept a standing army and there is no doubt that it certainly, helped in the rise of Magadha.

◆ The various powerful rulers of different dynasties contributed to the rise of Magadha. The foundation of the Magadha empire was laid down by Bimbisara and Ajatasatru. Both were ambitious rulers and extended the boundaries of Magadha both by war and diplomacy. "The accounts of the reign of Bimbisara and Ajatasatru" writes Dr A.L. Basham. "give evidence of a definite policy, aimed at the control of as much of the course of the Ganges as possible."

◆ Dr Basham also points out that the idea of a big empire

was picked up by Bimbisara and Ajatasatru from the example of Cyrus, the Great of Persia, who had become a ruler only sixteen years earlier than Bimbisara in Magadha and succeeded in building up Persia as the seat of one of the greatest empires of the world. He writes, "It is hardly likely that the kings of Magadha w ere ignorant of what was happening in the North-West. We believe that their expansionist policy was in part inspired by the example of Persians."

◆ The contention of Dr Basham definitely has practical wisdom but it is also a fact that Indian rulers had no compulsion to look to any foreign country for the ideal of an imperial kingdom. Rajasuya and Asvamedha ceremonies were performed by Indian rulers for the extension of their empires right from the later Vedic age onwards. After Ajatasatru, Sisunaga pursued the policy of empire-building and succeeded.

◆ Then came the Nandas who, finally, succeeded in establishing the first great empire in India. The Nanda rulers were Shudras. They were despotic rulers, who oppressed their subjects and collected enormous wealth in the state-treasury. Their rule, therefore, was unpopular which led to their weakness and contributed towards the downfall of their empire. Yet, the Nandas have their importance in Indian history. They created a most extensive empire in India and left it to their successors, the Mauryas in a position when it was extremely prosperous and militarily strong so that the Mauryas became powerful enough to turn the foreigners, the Greeks, out of India and also succeeded in completing the task began by Bimbisara and Ajatasatru of consolidating India in a big empire.

◆ Besides, the Nandas participated in weakening the caste-system during their time. Dr R.K. Mookerji writes: "The 5th and the 6th centuries B.C. hold out strange phenomenon before us. Kshatriya Chiefs founding popular religious sects which menaced Vedic religion and Shudra leaders establishing a big empire in Aryavarta on the ruins of Kshatriya kingdoms." Thus, the ambitious rulers of Magadha, its geographical location, fertility of its land, its minerals and forests and. thereby, its economic prosperity and liberal cultural traditions of the people of Magadha helped in its rise and in making it the first imperial power of India.

• **Bimbisara (544-493 B.C.)** : The rise of Magadha started with the accession of Bimbisara to its throne. He was a contemporary of Mahatma Buddha. Dr Bhandarkar has expressed the view that Bimbisara belonged to the Great Naga dynasty and was originally the commander-in-chief, probably of the Vajjis who once held sway over Magadha and, ultimately, succeeded in crowning himself as the king.But the Buddhist- texts give a different version. According to Asvaghosha's Buddhacharita, he belonged to Haryanka-kula and Mahavamsa refers that his father appointed him as king at the age of fifteen. Mahavamsa does not state the name of his father but according to other sources, he was named Bhattiya or Mahapadma.Bimbisara ruled for nearly forty-nine years. Its capital was Rajagriha. He was a man of determination and political foresight who realized the importance of a large kingdom and decided to make Magadha such a state. He pursued his ambition both by wars of conquest and a policy of matrimonial alliances.It has been said that he had five hundred wives. One may not agree with this number but it is certain that he entered into dynastic relations based on marriage with several important royal families of his time which helped him much in his political career.His first wife was a sister of Prasenajit, the king of Kosala who gave him a part of the kingdom of Kasi in dowry. His second wife was Chellana, daughter of the Lichchhavi king, Chetaka who was the most important feudatory chief of the republican state of the Vrijis with its capital of Vaisali.Another wife of his was Vasavi, princess of the kingdom of Vaideh and yet another, was Khema daughter of the king of Madra (Central Punjab). These marriage alliances definitely enhanced his prestige besides helping him in the extension of his territories.He was a successful diplomat as well. He maintained friendly relations not only with nearby strong states but also with distant powers. He sent his famous physician, Jivaka, to the neighbouring state of Avanti when its ruler, Chanda Pradyota fell ill and was, thus, able to maintain good relations with him. All this must have helped him in pursuing his policy for the extension of his kingdom.Bimbisara conquered the state of Anga. It was, probably, his only conquest but a very important one. Anga was a big and prosperous state at that time and its conquest marked the beginning of the greatness of Magadha. Bimbisara's father was defeated by Brahadatta. king of Anga. Probably, it was to avenge this defeat that Bimbisara attacked Anga and succeeded in conquering it.Bimbisara, for the first time, laid down the foundation of an efficient administration in Magadha. He constructed several canals and roads, appointed several new officers for administrative purposes and arranged for the regular collection of revenue. It helped him in increasing his financial resources and military strength. It is said that the kingdom of Magadha had 80,000 villages at that time. Bimbisara proved to be an able ruler who recognized the necessity of an efficient administration.There were several ministers who helped the king in administration. They were chosen on merit and their advice was generally not ignored. Besides, there were different officers who were divided into different categories according to the nature of their work. The executive or administrative officers were called Sambbatakas, the judicial officers Voharikas and the military officers Senanayakas.However, the basic units of administration were villages. Each village was under the jurisdiction of a headman who was responsible for the collection of taxes and handing them over to the other officials of the state. Theoretically, the land belonged to the king though nobody was displaced from the land till he paid 1/6th of the produce, which was regarded the king's share.Mostly Sudras worked as cultivators though they w ere not masters of the land. They were engaged as labourers. This had lowered their status. Therefore, a new class of Sudras, that is untouchables, came to be recognized during this period.Bimbisara was very much tolerant in religious affairs. He revered both Jainism and Buddhism equally. Therefore, both the Jainas and the Buddhists claimed Bimbisara as their follower.Bimbisara was killed by his own son Ajatasatru (Kunika). But the Jainas and the Buddhists have expressed different opinions regarding the episode of his death. According to Jaina texts Ajatasatru imprisoned his father but felt guilty afterwards and when he went to let him off, Bimbisara himself took poison out of fear and died. The Buddhist texts claim that Ajatasatru himself killed his father and he confessed this fact to the Buddha. Whatever might be the actual fact, it is certain that Ajatasatm was responsible for the death of his father and ascended his throne after him.

• **Ajatasatru (493-462 B.C.) :**Ajatasatru continued his father's policy of expansion through military conquests. First, a fierce struggle started between Magadha and Kosala. Prasenajit's sister who was the wife of Bimbisara died of grief at the death of her husband. Prasenajit could not tolerate it and asked Ajatasatru to return back Kasi which was given in dowry to Bimbisara.When it was refused by Ajatasatru, a protracted war began between Magadha and Kosala. The war remained indecisive for a long time but ultimately Prasenajit agreed to give Kasi to Ajatasatru and also gave his daughter Vajira in marriage to him, which proves that the outcome of war, finally, went in favour of Magadha.However, the foundation of the political supremacy of Magadha was laid by Ajatasatru by defeating the strong confederacy of Vriji. The confederacy which dominated Eastern India included 36 republican states, viz., 9 Mallaki, 9 Lichchhavi and 18 gana-rajyas of Kasi and Kosala. Various reasons have been assigned for this conflict between these two powers. The generally held belief that Padmavati, wife of Ajatasatru, incited him for this conflict seems to be less satisfactory.Jaina-texts state that two brothers of Ajatasatru, Halla and Vehalla, fled to Vaisal, the capital of the Lichchhavis, with the state-elephant of Magadha and a precious necklace given to 'hem by their father Bimbisara. The Lichchhavis refused to return the fugitives to Ajatasatru and therefore, he declared war against them.According to Buddhist-texts, the bone of contention between the two powers was a new-found jewel-mine. Both had agreed to share equally the jewels of the mine but Lichchhavis violated this agreement and so the war was declared by Magadha.These might be the immediate causes of the war but the basic cause seems to be different. The real issue was that Magadha could not be the supreme power in Eastern India unless this powerful confederacy was defeated. It was realised by both sides.That is why not only the Lichchhavis but the entire Vriji confederacy including the chiefs of Kasi and Kosala united themselves against Magadha. Dr D.N. Jha has given another reason of this conflict. He has opined that both the states claimed their rule over the river Ganges and the right to collect trade-tax from there. This led to their conflict.The conflict between Magadha and the confederacy continued for sixteen years (484-468 B.C.). Ajatasatru made all sorts of preparations for it. To be near the theatre of war, he built up a new fort near the bank of the Ganges, which later on gave rise to the famous city of Pataliputra and the future capital of Magadha. Ajatasatm also realised that he could not gain victory against such a powerful confederacy unless its inner unity was destroyed.Therefore, he sent one of his ministers, Vassakara, to sow seeds of dissension amongst the members of the confederacy. Vassakara remained there for three years and proved quite successful in his mission. The political and social unity of the Vrijis was broken. Besides, Magadha was able to produce two new weapons of war.One was the Mahasilakantaka which was used to throw heavy pieces of stone on enemy from a distance. The other was the Rathamusala, a chariot with knives and cutting edges fixed on to it and a place under cover for the charioteer. Thus, after preparing himself diplomatically and militarily, Ajatasatru attacked the Vrijis and finally won. This victory gave Magadha an unchallenged supremacy over East India.The success of Ajatasatru aroused the hostility of king Chanda Pradvota of Avanti who started making preparations to attack Magadha. But it was Ajatasatru who strengthened his fortifications and took various other measures to defend his boundaries and succeeded. Pradvota could not attack Magadha. Thus, Ajatasatru was successful in further extending the boundaries of his kingdom and in laying the foundations of the greatness of Magadha.Ajatasatru was of liberal religious opinions. Jaina-texts represent him as a Jain and Buddhist-texts as a Buddhist Ajatasatru. probably , was first inclined to Jainism but later on he became a devotee of the Buddha. The first General Council of the Buddhists was held under his patronage near Rajagriha. It is also believed that he built several Buddhist Chaityas.

• **The Successors of Ajatasatru (462-430 B.C.)** :Ajatasatm was succeeded by his son Udayabhadra. The rivalry between Magadha and Avanti continued during his time but Udayabhadra succeeded in defeating Palaka, the then ruler of Avanti several times. It is believed that Palaka then engaged a hired assassin to kill Udayabhadra who murdered him when he was listening to the discourse of a religious teacher. Udayabhadra was a Jaina. He built a town called Kusumapura and a Jain Chaityagriha inside it.Udayabhadra was succeeded by Anurudha, Munda and Nagadasaka respec-tively. None of them proved himself capable of ruling and according to Buddhist- texts each of them was a parricide. It created dissatisfaction among their subjects and therefore, one of the ministers of the last king, Sisunaga succeeded in overthrowing his rule and established the rule of a new dynasty.

- **Sisunaga and His Successors (430-364 B.C.)** :Sisunaga had gained respect under the weak successors of Ajatasatru and, probably, became the ruler of Magadha with the consent of the people. He proved to be a capable ruler and extended the territories of Magadha. The neighbouring rival state of Avanti, Vatsa and Kosala were defeated by him and their territories annexed to Magadha. Thus, he also contributed to the greatness of Magadha.Sisunaga was succeeded by his son Kalasoka or Kakavarna. He made Pataliputra the capital of Magadha. The second Buddhist General Council was held during his time at Vaisali. Kalasoka was murdered because of a palace conspiracy and, probably, his murderer was the founder of the Nanda dynasty.However, Mahavamsa says that the ten sons of Kalasoka ruled for ten years after him. Probably, the princes were allowed to rule nominally for these years to cover the guilt of the murder of their father. But, ultimately, all of them were killed and a new dynasty of kings started its rule over Magadha.

- **The Nanda Dynasty (364-324 B.C.)** :There is a difference of opinion with regard to the first Nanda ruler and his progeny. The Puranas call him Mahapadma while Mahabodhivamsa describes his name as Ugrasena. The Jain-texts describe him as the son of a barber while Puranas refer to him as 'the son of a king by a Sudra-woman.' Yet, it is certain that the founder of the Nanda dynasty was a Sudra.According to Puranas, Mahapadma Nanda destroyed all Kshatriya rulers. The kingdoms of Aikshvakus, Panchalas, Kasis, Haihayas, Kalingas, Asmakas, Kurus, Maithilas, Sursenas etc., were defeated and their territories were annexed to Magadha. There are a few evidences which suggest that the Nandas ruled over the southern part of Bombay and north-western part of Mysore. The evidences are not conclusive.Yet it is certain that the Nandas succeeded in establishing a great empire or rather the first one in the real sense which covered the greater part of northern India and also part of the South. And the credit for it goes primarily to the first ruler of this dynasty, Mahapadma Nanda.He completed the work which was started by Bimbisara, made Magadha the most extensive and powerful kingdom in India and ushered in the age of the Empire in this country. It is accepted by all that n ne rulers of the Nanda dynasty ruled over Magadha.However, while the Puranas state that the first Nanda was the father of the other eight Nandas, the Buddhist-texts take all the Nandas as brothers. Very little is known about the history of the Nandas after Mahapadma Nanda except the last ruler, nicknamed Dhana Nanda (the worshipper of Mammon).He was a contemporary of Alexander and his empire seems to have extended up to the frontiers of Punjab. He was a powerful king and kept a large army. But he was cruel and miserly. He accumulated fabulous wealth at the expense of his subjects by means of excessive taxation and exactions.Therefore, he was unpopular among his subjects. Another cause of his unpopularity must have been that he was a Sudra by caste. Chandra Gupta Maurya, the founder of the Mauryan dynasty, took advantage of his unpopularity and misgovernment, succeeded in killing him and captured the throne of Magadha.